EXTREME SPORTS BIOGRAPHIES ™

DAVE MIRRA

BMX Champion

Ian F. Mahaney

The Rosen Publishing Group's
PowerKids Press™
New York

To my favorite niece, Claire

Safety gear, including helmets, elbow pads, kneepads, shin guards, and gloves, should be worn while riding BMX.
Do not attempt tricks without proper gear, instruction, and supervision.

Published in 2005 by The Rosen Publishing Group, Inc.
29 East 21st Street, New York, NY 10010

First Edition

Editor: Heidi Leigh Johansen
Book Design: Mike Donnellan
Layout Design: Kim Sonsky
Photo Researcher: Peter Tomlinson

Cover, p. 8 © AP / Wide World Photos; pp. 4, 7, 11 (inset), 12, 16, 19 (right), 22 Getty Images; pp. 4 (inset), 20 © Duomo / CORBIS; p. 11 © Steve Boyle / NewSport / CORBIS; p. 15 Tony Donaldson / Icon SMI; pp. 15 (inset), 20 (inset) © Al Fuchs / NewSport / CORBIS; p. 16 (inset) © Shazamm; p. 19 (left) © Lutz Bongarts / SportsChrome USA.

Library of Congress Cataloging-in-Publication Data

Mahaney, Ian F.
Dave Mirra : BMX champion / Ian F. Mahaney.— 1st ed.
    v. cm. — (Extreme sports biographies)
Includes bibliographical references and index.
Contents: Extreme BMX — Getting to know Dave Mirra — BMX bikes — Dave gets competitive — Dave goes pro — The X Games — The Miracle Man — Dave's super tricks — BMX safety — Dave Mirra keeps busy.
ISBN 1-4042-2744-X (Library Binding)
1. Mirra, Dave, 1974—Juvenile literature. 2. Cyclists—United States—Biography—Juvenile literature. 3. Bicycle motocross—Juvenile literature. [1. Mirra, Dave, 1974– 2. Bicyclists. 3. Bicycle motocross.] I. Title. II. Series.

GV1051.M57M35 2005
796.6'2'092—dc22

2003025649

Manufactured in the United States of America

Contents

Dave Mirra, a world-famous BMX champion, jumps off a ramp and into the air in a freestyle course. "BMX" stands for "bicycle motocross." There are two main types of BMX biking, freestyle and racing. Dave Mirra likes freestyle the best. Inset: The BMX superstar takes a moment to relax on his bike.

Extreme BMX

Bicycle motocross (BMX) is an **extreme sport** in which people ride sturdy bicycles, or bikes, and **perform** daring tricks. BMX riders do tricks and race on **half-pipes** and on tracks with **ramps** and jumps. In the early 1970s, young bicyclists in California began copying **motorcycle** riders who performed tricks on dirt courses. The first bicycle **stunt** riders made **adjustments** to their bicycles to make them stronger. These riders rode on homemade dirt tracks with wooden ramps and dirt mounds. Soon BMX became a very popular extreme sport. Now some BMX riders race around tracks in racing events and others do tricks such as spinning the bike in midair in freestyle events. Dave Mirra is one of the best freestyle BMX **champions** in the world. He has helped to make the sport of BMX popular among many people around the world.

Getting to Know Dave Mirra

Dave Mirra was born in Chittenango, New York, on April 4, 1974. Chittenango is in central New York, about 20 miles (32 km) outside of Syracuse. When Dave was four years old, his parents, Linda and Mike, bought him a BMX bike. Dave rode his new bike as often as he could with his older brother, Tim. They built ramps so they could jump off them on their bikes and "catch air." Catching air is jumping into the air on your bike, using either an **obstacle** or your own strength. Dave watched older kids perform tricks on their bikes and tried to perform the same tricks. Dave learned tricks like the bunny hop 180. In a bunny hop 180, Dave jumps so that both wheels of his bike are in the air. Then he spins in midair so that he lands in the opposite direction from the one in which he was originally facing.

Dave performs a bunny hop 180, wearing all his safety gear, which includes a sturdy helmet. In a 180, the rider spins 180 degrees, or one-half of a circle, in the air. A 360-degree spin is a full circle.

Dave performs a twisting jump off an obstacle. He is holding on to the handlebars tightly and has only his left foot on the back peg of his bike.

BMX Bikes

Every bicycle is **designed** for a special purpose. Racing bikes, like the one that the **professional**, or pro, bicycle racer Lance Armstrong rides, are designed to go very fast. They are thin and have very light, large wheels. BMX bikes are designed to be sturdy and strong enough to withstand hard riding. BMX bikes have thick tires, sturdy rims and handlebars, and a strong frame. All of these important features allow BMX riders to make hard landings after jumping in the air. BMX **competitions** would not last long if the bikes were not strong. This is because BMX riders perform many hard tricks on their bikes.

Many BMX bikers make extra adjustments to their bikes. For example, some bikers put pegs, or strong metal parts, on each side of their bike wheels. They stand on the pegs while performing special tricks.

Dave Gets Competitive

In 1984, when Dave was 10, most BMX riders were racers. This means that they raced around dirt tracks that had mounds and jumps. The objective was to finish first. That year Dave entered a BMX racing competition in Ohio. Though he finished in second-to-last place, Dave did not give up hope or stop practicing. Dave loved riding and was a very **determined** child. He built bigger ramps and jumps in the front yard of his house. Dave practiced freestyle riding with his friends and his brother, Tim, because they could practice freestyle without a racetrack. Dave practiced on his homemade ramps until he learned to complete hard tricks. After entering several freestyle competitions, Dave caught the eye of a bike company called Haro. Haro began to **sponsor** Dave. That means that Haro paid for Dave to enter competitions and gave him free bikes and gear made by Haro.

Dave flies through the air on his bike in competition. As a child, Dave tried many other sports, including tennis and basketball, but none excited him like riding his BMX bike did. Inset: Dave signs his name for a young fan.

Dave catches air off the half-pipe. He turns his body to the side before diving full speed with his bike back onto the U-shaped surface of the half-pipe.

Dave Goes Pro

In 1992, at 18 years old, Dave had graduated from high school and was ready to direct all of his energy to the world of BMX. Dave became a professional BMX rider, which means that he began to earn a living by competing in BMX competitions. It was the best job Dave could imagine! He quit his job washing dishes and went on a BMX tour around the country. Dave was showing off his moves at competitions and making new friends and fans. Dave began to rule the BMX scene with his unbelievable and inventive BMX moves. More companies decided to sponsor him. Adidas, another sporting goods company, became Dave's sponsor and allowed him to design a new sports shoe. Dave also designed a Dave Mirra bicycle for Haro, which has his name on it. Kids all over the world ride Dave's bike!

The Miracle Boy

In December 1993, a drunk driver did not stop at a red light and the car hit Dave Mirra. At the hospital, Dave's doctors told him that he would never be able to ride his bike competitively again. However, Dave was determined to ride and to compete again. Dave's body had been badly hurt in the **accident**, but, after six months of rest, Dave was on his bike again. Dave was even performing stunts on the half-pipe! Dave's nickname is **Miracle** Boy. A miracle is a surprising and unusual event. People call Dave the Miracle Boy because he is able to complete very hard BMX tricks. Dave may also be called Miracle Boy because he got better so quickly after his bad accident.

ESPN chose Dave Mirra as the BMX Rider of the Year in 2001. This award honored Dave's sportsmanship, tricky moves, talent, and creativity.

Dave rides the half-pipe in a BMX event in California. Inset: Dave accepts his award after being voted BMX Rider of the Year in 2001 by the ESPN Action Sports & Music Awards.

Dave lifts his bike away from his legs in a midair trick. Dave has appeared on "Good Morning America," a TV show, and on the cover of Rolling Stone magazine. Inset: Dave, in yellow, accepts the 2002 silver medal in vert at the Gravity Games, another extreme sports event. He also won the 2002 gold in park.

The X Games

The X Games is an extreme sports competition that is held every year. The Summer X Games features BMX, skateboarding, in-line skating, and other extreme sports. In 1995, the first X Games was held. That year it was called the Extreme Games.

Dave Mirra has won more X-Games **medals** than anyone in the history of the X Games, with 18 medals, including 12 gold medals. Dave has been the most successful BMX rider in two X-Games BMX events, vert and park. "Vert" stands for **vertical** and is Dave's best event. In vert, riders perform tricks on a half-pipe. In park, riders bike on a course with obstacles like rails and ramps. Riders use the obstacles to catch air and to perform tricks and stunts. Dave won the gold medal in vert at the 2001 X Games. At the 2003 **Global** X Games, Dave took home the gold medal in park.

Dave's Super Tricks

One **miraculous** trick that the Miracle Boy performs is the double backflip. At the 2000 X Games, Dave rode up one side of an upside-down-V-shaped obstacle and flipped backward two times before landing and riding down the other side. This was the first-ever double backflip to be landed in competition.

BMX bikes have a feature called a rotor that prevents the bike's brakes from tangling when the rider spins the handlebars. The rotor helps Dave to perform one of his best-known tricks, called the 360 truck driver. In the 360 truck driver, Dave spins his bike around in a 360-degree circle while spinning the handlebars so it looks as if he is turning the wheel of a truck. Dave is also famous for performing tricks without holding the handlebars. Dave can flip his bike once, in a 360, and twice, in a 720, while only holding on to the bike with his legs!

Flipping once is called a 360 because the rider flips 360 degrees, or a full circle, in the air. Flipping twice is called a 720. Above Left: The Miracle Boy spreads his arms wide in a cool trick. Above Right: Dave performs a backflip.

Dave rides a steep obstacle. Inset: All BMX riders fall. Dave is no exception. Dave learned how to fall properly when he first started riding a bike. He always wears safety gear. Also, Dave tries never to fall on top of his bike. Instead, he pushes the bike away from his body if he is about to fall.

BMX Safety

BMX riding can be an unsafe sport. Dave Mirra has been hurt many times falling off his BMX bike. His most serious **injury** happened when he hurt his **spleen** at a competition in 1995. If a superstar like Dave can get hurt, anybody can. When riding on the half-pipe, BMX riders jump into the air at the top of the half-pipe, which is usually 12 feet (3.7 m) tall. If a rider jumps 5 feet (1.5 m) into the air off the top of the half-pipe, the rider is 17 feet (5.2 m) above the ground! A fall from that height could be very painful. Dave Mirra and all professional riders are careful and practice extreme safety. Dave always keeps his head safe by wearing a helmet when he rides his bike. Dave also wears elbow pads, kneepads, and sturdy gloves. Dave's falls do not hurt as much with strong pads to keep him safe.

Dave Mirra Keeps Busy

In 1995, Dave moved from central New York to Greenville, North Carolina, to be near his brother, Tim. Dave loves living in North Carolina and can practice his moves with the many other BMX riders who live in Greenville. Dave often rides in Greenville with his friend and fellow BMX rider, Ryan Nyquist. Dave loves to **golf** and to spend time doing **charity** work. Dave sponsors six children every summer to attend the Woodward Camp, an extreme sports summer camp in Pennsylvania. Dave has performed his moves in New Zealand, Malaysia, and Canada. In 2003, Dave won two gold medals in a BMX competition in Montpellier, France. Watch for Dave at the next X Games. There is no doubt that he will delight us for many years to come!

Glossary

accident (AK-sih-dent) An unexpected and sometimes bad event.

adjustments (uh-JUST-ments) Changes.

champions (CHAM-pee-unz) The best, or the winners.

charity (CHAR-ih-tee) Work done to help other people.

competitions (kom-pih-TIH-shinz) Games.

designed (dih-ZYND) To have planned the form of something.

determined (dih-TER-mind) Being very focused on doing something.

extreme sport (ek-STREEM SPORT) A bold and uncommon sport, such as BMX, in-line skating, motocross, skateboarding, snowboarding, and wakeboarding.

global (GLOH-bul) Having to do with the whole world.

golf (GOLF) A game played on a grass course with clubs and a small, hard ball.

half-pipes (HAF-pyps) Ramps that are shaped like a big *U*.

injury (IN-juh-ree) Harm done to a person's body.

medals (MEH-dulz) Small, round pieces of metal given as prizes.

miracle (MIR-ih-kul) A wonderful or unusual event outside the laws of nature.

miraculous (mih-RA-kyuh-lus) Incredible.

motorcycle (MOH-ter-sy-kul) A motorized bike.

obstacle (OB-stih-kul) An object that BMX riders use to perform tricks.

perform (per-FORM) To carry out, to do.

professional (pruh-FEH-shuh-nul) Paid for what he or she does.

ramps (RAMPS) Obstacles used by BMX riders to perform tricks.

spleen (SPLEEN) A part of the human body near the stomach.

sponsor (SPON-ser) To give gear and money to a sportsman or sportswoman.

stunt (STUNT) Trick.

vertical (VER-tih-kul) In an up-and-down direction.

Index

Web Sites

Due to the changing nature of Internet links, PowerKids Press has developed an online list of Web sites related to the subject of this book. This site is updated regularly. Please use this link to access the list: www.powerkidslinks.com/esb/mirra/

24